I0476017

HOW TO AVOID CAREER SUICIDE?

A Quick, Practical Guide to
Jump-Start a Great Career!

SUMAN V R

PARTRIDGE

To order additional copies of this book, contact
Partridge India
000 800 10062 62
orders.india@partridgepublishing.com

www.partridgepublishing.com/india

To

You,
who never stopped learning!
Me,
who never stopped trying!
Aanya, Anish, and Vivek,
my partners in crime every day! You are awesome!

Stay blessed and thank you!

CONTENTS

INTRODUCTION

You don't have to be great to start, but
you have to start to be great.

—Zig Ziglar

So LET'S JUMP IN! >>>>>

In your early twenties, the fabulous student life is done, and you are looking forward to a successful and satisfying career. But does this come true for all the talented and deserving young professionals? Not so; statistics prove that only a handful goes on to achieve tremendous success, while for others, life doesn't turn out like the way they had hoped.

I have always been intrigued by the question, why are some people more successful than others? The road to the answer to this question includes personal experience, extensive research, and inputs from people with more than twenty years' work experiences on what they would redo at the beginning of their career. The answer reconfirms the adage, 'We are *not* born with the traits needed for success. We can cultivate it over time with the *right attitude* and clearly defined *personal success statement*, which includes vision and purpose of our life.'

So the good news is that we all have the potential to be winners. Winners have imbibed in them many important characteristics like determination, motivation, perseverance, and integrity. However, the most important and the first step to achieve our potential is 'attitude'. You might think that this is nothing new as attitude is such an overused word in our lives, but it is deservingly so.

Attitude is everything!

The tricky part is to *ensure* that we actually have a positive attitude in challenging situations. In order to maintain a favorable self-image, people very rarely admit, even to themselves, that they have a negative attitude. Evaluating our attitude and building a positive attitude is 100 per cent within our control. Making positivity a habit takes work and a definite change in the mind-set.

History is full of several successful people like JK Rowling, Walt Disney, among others, who proved the major impact positive thinking and attitude has on our lives. Everything comes down to having a *positive attitude*. Zig Ziglar, an American motivational speaker, rightly said, 'Your attitude, not your aptitude, will determine your altitude.' However, all this positive thinking does *not* mean we ignore life's problems and challenges. It just means that we look at it more optimistically. This makes a world of difference.

In addition to positive attitude, having a defined 'personal success statement' is an important tool for personal development and a prerequisite for a long-lasting career. The reason for this is, 'How do you measure your success if you don't know what your success barometer is?'

Personal success statement is your success barometer.

Success means different things for different people. Not everyone in the world wants a fancy job, big house, and big car. So what's your success statement? If you don't have your own success definition, you may end up identifying with someone else's success definition. In this case, there is a higher risk of feeling like a failure when you don't measure up. This will lead to anxiety, burnout, and dejection. Hence, build your success statement with *only* your vision, happiness, and fulfillment in mind.

For many of us, 'career' is by far the biggest contributor for our feelings of success and achievement. However, a 'balanced life' approach is more suitable in the long run. In addition to career, this statement should include all aspects of our lives like spiritual, health, and relationships.

Building this statement provides an opportunity to look at our values and beliefs. It forces us to think clearly on questions like, What is important to me? What does success mean to me? What is my life's work? It provides a sense of direction and focus instead of *unconsciously going through life*. The additional advantage is it helps to make a decision in conflicting situations. I have personally used my success statement to resolve bandwidth conflicts and prioritize my business and family commitments.

Right off the bat, let's spend some time to think clearly and write a few well-thought-of lines. Just to give an idea, some sample lines are as follows: *I want to challenge myself with yoga as health is a priority / I want to finish PMP certification as management is my goal / I want to learn new things every day / Integrity and honesty are my core strengths, and all my actions should reflect it / Family above everything else.*

Build Your Personal Success Statement:

Things change every day, so will our expectations, thinking, and priorities. This will certainly have an impact on our career, vision, and relationships. It's imperative to consider these changes and readjust the statement annually. Without tracking the statement regularly over the years, the whole exercise will be futile.

The strength of a building lies in its foundation. Likewise, our attitude and success statement provide us with the strength to achieve success in this ever-changing world. In addition to this, the subsequent sections in the book provide practical and necessary tips that can help boost your career. Incorporating these topics in your personal development needs time and commitment. Hence, pick one topic in the beginning and work on it. Any success from this one will encourage you to incorporate more tips.

PROFESSIONAL NETWORKING

The richest people in the world look for and
build networks; everyone else looks for work.
—Robert Kiyosaki

What is networking?

Networking is a self-explanatory buzzword and is a crucial skill for any professional. As we get into details, the one definition that's best suited is **using the existing or building new professional contacts to help advance your career**. Networking can be used as leverage for career growth / job opportunities / business partnerships. The crux of networking is to 'build relationships'.

Networking activity helps you to put your best foot forward, increase visibility, ensure that other people know who you are and what you do. This doesn't need a formal environment or an event. It could be as casual as a business conversation with a colleague in between a busy day. The primary purpose of this activity should always be to develop mutually beneficial long-term business relationships and build the trust factor.

Networking is building trust and
long-term relationships!

Richard Branson, founder of the Virgin group, has quoted, 'Business is all about personal contact. No matter how heavy your workload is . . . everyone can and should be a networker.' He insists everyone on his staff to be well versed in this skill. He also credits this as a reason that helped Virgin expand into so many different industries from music to mobile phone services.

Why do we need to network?

According to 2017 LinkedIn global survey results, almost 80 per cent of professionals consider networking to be important for career success. And more importantly, 70 per cent of people in 2016 were hired at a company where they had a contact. These statistics clearly shows the importance of networking in your career and proves beyond doubt that networking matters in the long run as employers prefer to hire through contacts and referral programs. If you are an entrepreneur, networking helps you meet potential clients or partnerships to expand your business in new areas.

In addition to referrals and new business opportunities, networking is great in finding a mentor. A mentor can provide knowledge, encouragement, and advice to propel your professional growth. Having a mentor, especially in the early stages of your career, will immensely help in decisions, strategy, and focus. In office or networking events, you should connect with various people and study and evaluate their work before choosing them as your mentor.

Networking is vital during bad times in your career. It will help immensely when you are in desperate need for a job / new clients / startup funding. The general perspective when you are fired from your job is that you are not good at it. However, your contacts will have a better idea of your abilities and can help you bounce back sooner. Hence, networking should be your career cornerstone. However, an important point to remember is 'a reliable network *cannot* be built in a day', and if it's not nurtured, you may not have it when you need it.

Going back to LinkedIn statistics, majority (79 per cent) globally agrees that professional networking is valuable for career progression. However, less than half (48 per cent) globally says they keep in touch with their network when things are going well in their career. This is a huge red flag because if your career takes a downturn, there is no support to get it back on track as soon as possible. Nurturing long-term relationships is an important success mantra.

> Networking is a major support when
> your career takes a downturn.

How to network?

It's one thing to know that networking is important. It's a whole other thing to actually use it for career advancement. This is because for a lot of people, including me, networking doesn't come naturally; we have to step outside our comfort zone to actively build relationships. Hence, it's the most underused professional success skill.

Like other important attributes, this skill also can be mastered. Below are some of the little things that you can start off with, which will go a long way in forming a strong network:

1. Consistently stay in touch

    This is one of the simplest networking principles. Keep in touch with ex-colleagues, old friends, or contacts. Nothing fancy, it could be a short phone call, a simple message, or birthday wishes. This will keep you current in their minds and makes it easier when you have to call in for a favor.

    Reiterating, a trustworthy professional network cannot be built in a day. It must be nurtured consistently from the start of the career. We all get busy and lose touch with our contacts. To avoid this, set reminders to stay in touch with your connections regularly. If possible, make an effort to meet face-to-face. This helps in building trust in a relationship.

2. LinkedIn and other professional networking sites

    Register with the networking sites; LinkedIn is the most popular one. Ensure to spend time and effort to write a good career summary and career details on LinkedIn. Most importantly, be active on it—join job forums and groups, and connect with people with shared interests. This is especially useful for introverts as they have difficulty networking face-to-face. In addition to individuals, companies also use LinkedIn for recruiting and sharing information about the company. Using LinkedIn effectively has proven to be good for developing your network.

3. Give and you will receive

    Networking is not only about how it will help you, but also about going that extra mile to help others reach their goals. The golden rule in networking is that 'you must help and give to others before you can receive'. This will eventually help you improve your communication skills, be a team player, and collaborate with others. In addition, it will help hone your leadership skills, as helping others advance is a big part of being a good leader.

4. Attend events

    Attending networking events is a career booster. However, it can be intimidating even for the extroverts among us. Stepping outside your comfort zone to attend events is hugely beneficial as it helps in meeting like-minded individuals and improves your self-confidence.

    Connecting with experts from different fields who are invited to these events will help you stay up-to-date on the trends and help plan your future. It's important to note that it's essential to stay in touch with the people you have met in events. Otherwise, the whole exercise will be a waste of time.

5. Prioritize valuable contacts (inner circle)

    We live in a busy world; it's not feasible to maintain deep quality relationships with all the contacts in your network. Based on your success statement, prioritize your contacts and develop an inner circle with five to seven important connections/mentors. This will help you to meaningfully engage with these people.

This doesn't mean that you should disengage or discard other contacts, as they may become relevant in the future. For now, keep the involvement minimal, for example, email once a month as opposed to face-to-face meeting with the inner circle.

DISCOVER YOUR STRENGTHS

Success is achieved by developing our strengths,
not by eliminating our weaknesses.
—Marilyn vos Savant

What are your 'core strengths'?

It is important in your life and career to understand oneself and know what your strengths are. Core strengths are your capabilities, which come easily to you, and you are good at it. This will be the key to your success as it helps you leverage your capabilities to the maximum. On the flipside, everyone has weaknesses, and identifying your weaknesses will help you manage them. The most successfully used approach to career progression is to channel your energies on developing your strengths and learn to reduce the impact of your weaknesses on your career.

Understanding 'core strengths' is not limited to workplace skills/talent but includes personality as well. We need to discover our fundamental success traits like communication skills, people skills, problem-solving skills, planning skills, leadership skills, and personal traits like integrity, empathy, and enthusiasm among others. This assessment will definitely take time and effort, but it's an essential career investment.

Proven Success Mantra:
- Identify your strengths and weaknesses
- Develop your strengths
- Reduce the impact of your weaknesses

To make a difference, apart from discovering your strengths and weaknesses, it's vital to 'play to your strengths' too. The numerous researches in positive psychology have confirmed that applying your strengths in everyday life is important for your personal happiness and success. **Only when we put our strengths in practice we feel energized and at our best.** This helps productivity and has a positive impact on our lives.

Why know your strengths?

Knowing your strengths is essential for your personal development and growth. Abraham Maslow (1908–1970), an American psychologist, is well-known for creating Maslow's hierarchy of needs and popularizing the concept of self-actualization. Self-actualization is defined as 'the realization or fulfillment of one's talents and potentialities, especially considered as a drive or need present in everyone'. In simple terms, it means that every person aspires to reach their goals and fulfill their potential. Discovering and leveraging your strengths is one of the key areas in self-actualization. It helps in maximizing your potential and expanding your horizons. This in turn leads to a higher degree of self-fulfillment and happiness.

Furthermore, understanding your strengths will help focus your energy. In the beginning of my career, I was advised to identify my weaknesses and improve/work on that. With experience, I find it is not a good approach as you are not taking advantage of your strengths and shifting focus from what you are really good at.

The better approach is to **understand, improve, and leverage your strengths to the maximum and manage your weaknesses.** This has been proven time and time again. Michael Jordan was cut from his high school basketball team. Instead of giving up his dream, he realized that his strength was basketball, and he practiced every day rigorously till he made the team and became one of the most successful basketball players. Same with the Beatles; a label saying that 'guitar groups are on their way out' initially rejected them. However, it didn't take long for the Beatles to succeed as they played on their strengths.

There are many such examples. Channeling your energy on your strengths maximizes your personal development. This doesn't mean ignoring your weaknesses. Weaknesses needs to be managed to ensure that it doesn't hold you back. Continuous, focused effort on eliminating your weaknesses is not required; being good enough so that it doesn't negatively impact your career should suffice.

How to discover your strengths?

This is a very vast subject; let's start by discussing briefly about some aspects of this. First and foremost is self-assessment. Everyone should take the responsibility of knowing his or her strengths and weaknesses. This will take a great deal of self-awareness and self-reflection to become aware of what you are good at and are naturally inclined to do.

Strengths in the workplace skills category can be figured out by having couple of years of work experience, revisiting previous job assignments, and paying attention to the tasks/challenges in your job that makes you energized. Questions like, 'What do I enjoy most at work?' 'What am I most successful at?' will help identify the activities that you are instinctively drawn to and are highly productive at them. These activities give a feeling of achievement, satisfaction, and fulfillment after completing it and help identify your strengths.

Discovering fundamental personality traits requires insights into your personality, values, and motivations. It's hard to look at ourselves objectively, making this process difficult. In addition to self-awareness, there are standardized tests like Myer-Briggs personality types (MBTI), Gallup's Strengths Finder, and Richard Step Strengths and Weaknesses Aptitude Test (RSWAT) that help understand your core strengths and the right fit in terms of career/roles.

Objective self-assessment and self-awareness leads to self-mastery, and this is the True Power.

We are usually our own worst critics. Hence, in addition to self-assessment, it is advisable to ask feedback from other people who work with you and know you. The best way to do this is through a tool called Reflected Best Self Exercise (RBSE) developed by researchers Jane Dutton, Gretchen Spreitzer, Laura Morgan Roberts, and Robert Quinn. In this feedback-seeking exercise, you gather feedback from others in the form of narrative stories about when you performed at your best. You then integrate the stories submitted by colleagues, friends, and family members to create a portrait of your best self and a plan to leverage your strengths.

One thing is for sure: successful people are aware of their strengths at the beginning of their career and know how to channel it. Given the importance of this, a technique called SWOT (Strength, Weakness, Opportunities, Threat) analysis is included in all performance evaluation and hiring process. In addition to strengths and weaknesses, SWOT analysis also helps you identify the best opportunities that are available to you and the threats you face in reaching your goals.

Below is an example of personal SWOT analysis:

- Strengths: Good in management skills, fast learner, good communication skills.
- Weaknesses: Poor stress management skills, low self-confidence.
- Opportunities: Can apply for executive MBA program on company scholarship, can apply for a full management position at ABC Company.
- Threats: Colleague A is also applying for the MBA program, ABC Company wants to hire only MBA graduates.

Completing your SWOT analysis helps you identify gaps in your plan and utilize your talent to the fullest extent. It's important to note that the tools and techniques discussed above are from a ten-thousand-foot view. Detailing more on this topic will lead us offtrack from the subject of this book. The further reading section has excellent book references for anyone who wants to delve deeper into this topic.

PERSONAL PLAN

Plan your work for today and every
day, then work your plan.

—Margaret Thatcher

What is a personal development plan?

A well-aware 'success statement' is essential for personal development plan. Success statement acts as a goal and purpose based on which the plan will be defined. The other inputs to the plan include opportunities, strengths, values, life's priorities, and realities. As previously mentioned, you will require a high degree of self-awareness and introspection for this activity.

The most common mistake with this planning is that it gets limited to 'career planning'. Career is such a big part of life and success definition that usually personal plan will be just career strategy plan. We look for answers for work-related questions like, 'Where do I want to end up in five years?' or, 'What's my dream job?' And the rest of life works on autopilot. However, when life's priorities change, it can derail the whole system. Career cannot be planned in itself. It is a part of your life, not life itself.

Hence, the right approach is to plan your life as 'one complete unit'. This would include **your career, health, personal development, relationships, and fun/travel**. Even a simple question like, 'Where should I live?' can have both personal and professional implications. By planning with all the priorities in mind, you will save a lot of stress later.

Naysayers will not agree to the concept of life planning, saying life doesn't work as planned and things change. Studies show that having a personal plan that acts as a blueprint of what you want to achieve in your life will give you a better chance at success and personal fulfillment.

Plan your life, not just your career!

Why is personal planning required?

We all have our priorities and goals in life and career; most of the time we work on them unconsciously. It's easy to get distracted from what you want to achieve. The successful approach is to consciously develop a personal plan for a set period of time, i.e., two-year personal plan, and implement your goals. Plan is like a map in life. Personal plan helps you maintain focus and organize your personal goals. It makes you accountable to achieve those goals in the planned time period.

In addition to providing the right direction, it helps in motivation. The goals that are challenging and measurable provide a sense of achievement on completion. This translates into improved self-esteem and confidence to maximize your potential. As rightly quoted by Benjamin Franklin, 'If you fail to plan, you plan to fail.'

Personal planning helps in decision making and controlling the desired outcomes in life. When opportunity knocks, how will you handle it?

For example, 'When you were an undergraduate, you had a goal that you will continue to study further and complete your MBA.' However, a good job opportunity comes your way. What will be your decision? This decision could change your life direction. This is where a plan comes in. If you have a good plan in place, you can always go back to see your goals and the reason for it. This will help you make an informed decision and keep an eye on the bigger picture.

How do I build a personal plan?

If you are already a planner like myself, this section might seem repetitive. However, a quick glance might still help you tweak your system. For newbies, this planning process may seem long and tedious. Rest assured, it will become a habit after a few iterations. So let's get started!

The foremost thing to note in planning is that the time period for your personal development goals should be one to two years at the maximum. In this transitional world with distractions and challenges, there is a higher probability of realizing a goal with a one-year timeline than a goal with a five-year timeline. This is not meant to discourage long-term thinking; your vision and success statement gives the necessary aim and guidance for creating goals. The ideal strategy is to 'have a long-term vision but set goals with a one-year timeline and revisited the plan annually'.

There is no plan without goals. You can start building the plan by adding goals based on what you want to achieve. The goals should be well thought of and based in reality. If your personal circumstance does *not* support that goal, adding it will only result in failure even before you start. It should be challenging and also feasible. Few sample goals are as follows: learn to speak in Mandarin, get a master's degree in literature, or publish a book. It is highly recommended that you add SMART goals.

SMART goal in a self-development context means Specific, Measurable, Achievable, Relevant, and Time-bound goals. SMART goals are extensively used in the corporate world. Its first known use was by George T. Doran in his paper for an issue of *Management Review*. It can be customized for personal development plan as setting a broad-based goal like, 'Get into top management position in five years', and planning to 'write some certifications' to achieve the goal is not enough. SMART goals will help clearly define the objective, thereby increasing the success rate of goal completion. Sample SMART goal for the same example will be as follows:

- Specific: I want to write management certifications starting with PMP to improve my credibility for the top management position.
- Measurable (success criteria): 70 per cent score on all the certifications.
- Achievable: Yes, with my background experience in management, this is achievable.
- Relevant: Yes, it's the right time to work on the goal as the promotion interviews are scheduled in six months.
- Time-bound: Complete PMP in 3 months' timeframe.

As discussed earlier, ensure that the goals cover all important life areas: career, finance, health, personal growth, social relationships, and travel/fun. It's not possible to work on a goal in isolation. Channeling your energies to complete a goal in one area will have repercussions on other areas as well. Going back to the earlier example, if you have a family, working on achieving your management goal will affect your relationships goals. General well-being and life satisfaction can be achieved only when you pay attention to all areas of your life during goal setting.

Why do you want to achieve this goal? The thought process for this should be detailed out in the plan. This is a necessary motivator and a reality check. This will help you later when you relook/change the plan. For example, if your goal is to learn Mandarin, the reasons for it may be many such as improve career prospects, personal development, or impress someone. So 'Why?' has to be included in the plan to know the basis for adding the goal.

The result of the above will be a list of goals and the reason why you want to achieve it. Now, it's time to prioritize as taking up all the goals together may backfire. The goals should be prioritized based on your personal and professional commitments. Review how much time you have left every day to invest in self-development. Based on this, pick only one to two goals that you can focus on and complete it in the set timeframe. Successful accomplishment of the initial goals will improve your self-confidence to progress further.

Once there is clarity on the goal, the next step is, 'How?' What is the action plan to complete this goal? A goal is nothing but an idea until you have clear path to achieve it. The goal is then drilled down further to create specific clearly defined action items. Action items should have specific timelines, and it must be tracked to ensure that you are in the right direction to complete the goal. For instance, if the goal is to 'publish a book', the action item will be, 'finish manuscript by April 2018'.

Success criteria for a goal have to be identified before you start working on that goal. This makes the goal measurable. If your goal was to 'lose weight', is 2-pound weight loss considered successful or 10 pounds? Defining the success criteria beforehand is a motivator and entitles you to reward yourself for all the hard work for goal accomplishment.

Monitoring your goals is a nonnegotiable step in personal development plan. Without tracking your progress, all the time and effort spent on developing your plan will be worthless. Action items have to be tracked weekly and monthly till they are completed. In this digital age, it's a good idea to use the technology support for tracking like apps, calendars, and to-do lists. This makes it easy to evaluate progress.

End of the year is a good time to review the complete personal development plan. Celebrate your achievements and learn from your mistakes. Brainstorm and replan for the coming year, keeping in mind the lessons learnt and changing personal priorities. One good way to ensure that the plan is ready is to include and track your New Year resolutions in the personal development plan. A well-thought-of plan is a great way to kickstart the New Year.

Personal Development Plan:
- Define life goals
- Why the goal?
- Prioritize goals
- Success Definition
- Action plan
- Set timelines
- Track progress

The example below gives an idea on building a personal plan. You can customize it the way you see fit and easy to follow.

Personal Plan

Life Area : Career					
Goal	Why?	Success Definition	How? Action Items	End date	Completed?
Get certified in PMP	Will be an added advantage for manager promotion	Above 70% score	Start studying	30 Jun 2018	
			Attend training	11 Aug 2018	
			Mock test	21 Sep 2018	
			Certification	28 Sep 2018	
Life Area : Health					
Goal	Why?	Success Definition	How? Action Items	End date	Completed?
Lose 10 pounds	To keep type 2 diabetes in check	Weighing scale reading	Join gym	30 Sep 2018	
			Eat right	Ongoing	
Life Area : Personal Growth					
Goal	Why?	Success Definition	How? Action Items	End date	Completed?
Learn Mandarin	Promotion. Company opening a new branch in China.	1. To be able to speak in Mandarin 2. To be able to read Mandarin	To be decided after completing above two prioritized goals		

26

Potential Personal Plan Threats

A good plan depends on visualizing and forecasting the future. Yes, reiterating, not everything can be planned and controlled, but there is a better chance of success with planning. Based on experience, the following are the things that can ruin even a well-laid plan. We need to keep an eye out for these in decision-making process:

- **Money motivation**

  Money is one of the most important motivator for work. We cannot deny this as almost everyone works for money, unless you are wealthy and don't need a paycheck. Let's consider a scenario: Company A offers you a job with great paycheck, but the work is not so challenging. Company B offers you a job with lesser paycheck, but the work is challenging and will be good for your career. What will be your motivation for choosing the company? The motivator for choosing a job is different for different people. Apart from money, some of the other motivators are career progression, accomplishing personal development and vision, good social network, empowering people, etc. Select your motivator wisely as your career depends on it.

- **Keeping up to date with latest trends**

  We live in a fast-changing world. No matter in which industry you work in, it's important to keep up to date on news and trends. Your current job may not require it or encourage it, but it's crucial to include this in your plan and put it into action. There are different ways to go about this: attend events, seminars, online newsletters, forums, articles and opinions on social media from thought leaders, reading books. The time and effort put into this will definitely provide you the competitive edge that you are looking for.

- **Assumptions about children and marriage**

    Marriage and having kids are called life-changing decisions for a reason. They are indeed happy events but can have a huge impact on your personal and professional commitments, especially the role of family caregiver. We are living in a fool's paradise if we assume the earlier personal plan will not derail.

    There are various issues that can potentially crop up like change in location, coping with additional personal responsibility, time crunch, and additional economic burden. The exercise of 'visualizing the future' with all the possible scenarios and outcomes will help iron out some of these issues to reduce the negative impact on the career.

- **Working with relatives / close friends**

    This is a double-edged sword. There are advantages of working with family members / spouse, such as, they will willingly contribute for reduced salary during a downturn/startup, high trust and credibility factor, but in reality, it's been proven to have more disadvantages and challenges. The failure in professional relationship can cause a huge dent in the personal one; hence, this is not the decision to jump in blindly. Ensure that you have weighed the pros and cons clearly before you go for it.

- **Being an entrepreneur**

Ninety per cent or more working professionals dream of being an entrepreneur at some point in their career. The allure of becoming your own boss is hard to resist. This dream can easily become a nightmare if not planned and executed properly. Apart from the business plan for the new venture, your personal development plan should also include this aspect. Being an entrepreneur is a major life change and affects all areas of your life:

Personal Development – During the startup stages, you will be involved in all areas of your business: market research, planning, execution, human resources, and accounting. Well, you get the idea. Plan to attend some courses or work in a startup to learn the tricks of the trade.

Finance – You may need to bootstrap your business. In addition, the business may not make profit in the initial couple of years, and you have to be ready to sustain your life with minimum cost of living.

Relationships – You will be solely responsible for your business. Hence, the concept of work-life balance will not apply in the initial years, as you will be working doubly hard to get the business of the ground. This may take a toll on the family/relationships.

Health – If not monitored properly, the stress of getting a business off the ground may affect your health, and this will be counterproductive. Hence, it's important to take care of yourself in addition to your business.

Building a business from scratch is not an easy task. As per statistics, 50 per cent of new businesses fail within the first five years. In order to avoid failure, strategic business plan as well as a solid personal plan will act as a reliable blueprint. Your personal and business progress depends on this.

TIME MANAGEMENT

Time management is a misnomer the
challenge is to manage ourselves.

—Stephen Covey

What is time management?

Time management can be defined as the process of consciously planning the amount of time spent on specific activities in a day. It's an important skill to master early in life. Many people feel that twenty-four hours is not enough and spend their day running frenziedly from one activity to the other, achieving far less than planned. But in the same amount of time, successful people manage to outperform. The credit for this goes to good time management skills as it helps to organize your work, increase efficiency, and reduces stress.

A time management technique for work-life balance is the ultimate guideline that we all search for. In the recent years, advances in technology like video chat, email, smartphones, and provisions like work from home have contributed to further blur the boundary between work and life. This added use of technology could be beneficial if it is accessed when required. Else, the stress of being connected all the time will affect the physical and mental well-being of a person.

It's all about getting the right balance between various aspects of life: work, family, social life, and yourself. This is easier said than done. The plan should include adequate amount of time for the activities to nurture all life areas. Orison Swett Marden, an American author, has rightly noted, 'Work, love, and play are the great balance wheels of man's being.'

In the hustle and bustle of everyday life, it's very easy to ignore the time for your own needs. Scheduling time for yourself *every day* is a necessity to regenerate and reassess. You have twenty-four hours in a day. How do you want to spend it? This depends only on *you*. Time management helps you take control of your time and make the best use of it.

Do not forget to schedule *'me'* time every day to regenerate and reassess!

Why do we need time management?

There are many compelling reasons as to why time management is essential every day. Unless you fully understand the advantages, application of this skill will be minimal. Time is limited; this cannot change. However, you can control the ways in which you use this resource to your advantage.

As you progress in life, responsibilities and challenges increase. Time management techniques in everyday life will provide the requisite time to prioritize your task list and enable you to work on what's important and not what's urgent. In addition, this will avoid the 'firefighting' approach of running from one urgent task to another, overwhelmed with the amount of work that you have to do. You will feel more in control of your life rather than just going with the flow. This in turn reduces stress and helps you stay calm because the day is well planned and the challenges are anticipated.

Peter Drucker, the founder of modern management, in his book *The Effective Executive* has quoted, 'Efficiency is doing things right; effectiveness is doing the right things.' Time management skill ensures that you make conscious decisions to use your time effectively on important tasks. This reduces wasted time and effort, in turn increases your productivity, and you will be able to accomplish more with less time and effort.

Not using this skill is one of the major reasons of 'burnout' early in the career. Burnout is usually due to overwhelming constant stress from one's job. This could happen to anyone, a corporate employee who is under pressure due to continuous deadlines or a caregiver who is handling multiple responsibilities like kids, aging parents, etc. As per experts, the good way to avoid this is by taking control of your time by evaluating priorities, scheduling time with family/friends, and investing time for yourself every day. In other words, time management!

How to build a time management strategy?

In order to put together a time management strategy, it's essential to 'know how you spend your time every day'. If required, create a time log, which is a written record to track the tasks on which you spend your time. After a few days, analyze these logs to help identify the tasks that consume the most amount of time. Pareto principle, the 80/20 rule, can be applied here. This principle is named after the Italian economist Vilfredo

Pareto who stated that 80 per cent of the effects come from 20 per cent of the causes. Applying this to time management means '80 per cent of the tasks take up just 20 per cent of the time'. The remaining 20 per cent of the tasks take up 80 per cent of the time; these are the tasks that need to be improved upon to increase your effectiveness. Small steps every day will help you achieve the big goals that were thought impossible at the start.

Time logs help you analyse how you spend your time.

The time we have every day needs to be allocated among work responsibilities, action items in personal development plan, and other family/social commitments. The obvious next question is, how to manage all this? Instead of complex plans, the best technique that's proven to work is a simple 'daily to-do list'. The point to stress here is that the tasks in the to-do list should be at a micro-level, and task status update should be binary, i.e., either yes or no. This makes it easy to track your accomplishments at the end of the day. For example, if the goal is *'Get certified in PMP in 2018'*, action item will be *'Finish studying by April 2018'*, the entry in the daily to-do list will be *'Finish chapter 10'*. The order of the list is equally important. The list should start with the high-priority/important tasks, and these tasks should be tackled at the beginning of the day.

The list should be updated throughout the day to ensure that you are on track. Due to technology, there are plenty of planning tools available to create and update the tasks. Experts suggest that the time for assessment should be at end of the day every day. This daily session helps you check the accomplishments of the day and plan for the next day. A day well planned is a day well lived.

In addition, you have to consider your habits and working routine. What is your most productive time during the day? Different people prefer different timings, location, or environment to work. Habits can make you or break you. Hence, this has to be considered while creating a time management strategy.

There are some simple tips and tricks that can help you stay the course:

- **Assign priorities**

    Even the best-laid plans go haywire, as every day is different. The contingency plan for this is to assign priorities for the activities in the to-do list every day. As discussed, it's advisable to complete two to three 'most critical' items on the list early in the day. Alternatively, you can use the Eisenhower's urgent/important principle to complete the activities in the most effective way.

    Eisenhower's urgent/important principle helps prioritizing activities based on urgency and importance. Urgent activities are the ones that require immediate attention, and important activities are the ones that help us achieve our goals. This concept schedules the activities by putting them in four categories: (a) Important and Urgent; (b) Important and Not Urgent; (c) Not Important and Urgent; and (d) Not Important and Not Urgent. Whichever way you chose to do it, assigning priorities is important for the success of your strategy.

- **Delegating tasks**

    This is one of the key skills of a successful leader, and it will help you maximize your time. In order for this to be effective, you have to know to delegate the right tasks to the right people. It cannot always be a 'one-person show'; there will be times when you will need to include other people as that's the *best* use of your time. Delegating tasks along with responsibilities will empower and motivate the other person to complete the task successfully, and it will help you develop coaching and mentoring skills.

- **Minimize distractions**

    In this day and age, there are numerous activities that cause distractions at work—social media sites, playing games on smartphones, accessing entertainment sites, online shopping, WhatsApp, and replying to personal messages/ mails. Though, it looks like it doesn't take up a lot of time, in reality, it is actually a 'time-sink' and leads to lower productivity. As per recent studies, 'an employee could be spending more than two hours every day on activities unrelated to the job'. Hence, it's crucial to start paying attention to the time spent on these distractions. Instead of being always available, plan specific times in a day to catch up to these activities. This will help you work uninterrupted on the task on hand and minimize distractions.

• **Art of saying NO**

'When and how to say no' is a fine skill to develop early in the career. You get a lot of requests for your time at work—invitations, meetings, ideas, brainstorming session, etc. Our time is valuable, and just saying yes to requests without prioritization and understanding how it will add value to your day will topple your time management strategy. Learning to say no consciously, nicely, and politely without offending the other person is the best time management tool. Instead of giving an instant answer, a response like, 'I'll check and get back to you', will help you prioritize and manage your time better.

EMOTIONAL INTELLIGENCE (EI)

If your emotional abilities aren't in hand, if you don't
have self-awareness, if you are not able to manage
your distressing emotions, if you can't have empathy
and have effective relationships, then no matter how
smart you are, you are not going to get very far.

—Daniel Goleman

What is emotional intelligence (EI)?

Experts have defined *emotional intelligence* as the ability of a person to recognize, understand, and manage our own emotions as well as the emotions of others. In other words, being aware of the powerful effects of our emotions and to use this awareness to guide our behavior and impact and influence other people. Psychologists have been studying EI from as early as 1960s. However, this term and concept was made popular and accessible by Daniel Goleman in his book *Emotional Intelligence – Why It Can Matter More Than IQ* (1995).

People with high EI have the ability to respond quickly, solve the problem, and take good decisions even when they are under pressure. They are known to be good listeners and are able to help others with their problems. They know themselves well, trust their intuition, and handle criticism well as they believe it will help them with personal progress. This shows that EI is the basis for a lot of crucial skills we use every day. Hence, EI is a valuable 'intangible' skill to have in any situation and works as a 'differentiating' factor, providing you a much-needed edge in career growth. Even if you feel you don't have these skills, experts have concluded that these are not inborn talents but abilities that can be learnt, practiced, and developed.

The terms *emotional intelligence* (EI) and *emotional quotient* (EQ) have been used interchangeably for the past thirty years. In the industry, the term EQ is used in parallel with IQ as a measure or assessment of a person's emotional development, i.e., EI. There are many tests to measure EQ like Mayer-Salovey-Caruso Emotional Intelligence Test (MSCEIT), the Emotional Quotient Inventory 2.0 (EQ-i2.0), EQ-360. However, having a standard test for EQ is proving more challenging than IQ, and there is a lot of research still under way on this subject.

> Emotional intelligence is not an inborn trait but can be developed by practice and training.

Why do we need emotional intelligence?

Several studies have shown that people with higher emotional intelligence have a greater rate of success in most things they do. This is proven by the emotional intelligence statistic by Dr Travis Bradberry. He indicates '90 per cent of the top performers have high EQ' and 'EQ is responsible for 58 per cent of your job performance'. Higher emotional intelligence boosts career success, entrepreneurial potential, and leadership skills. It leads to higher levels of happiness, emotional and physical health, and improved social relationships.

This is due to the fact that career and life success does not only depend on intelligence and talent. There are other skills at play, like clear thinking and problem-solving skills under pressure, to work collaboratively with others by empathizing, motivating, influencing, or negotiating as necessary. These abstract skills are a part of emotional intelligence skill sets and are very much required in everything we do every day.

It's common knowledge that a person's EQ impacts his leadership abilities. High EQ is a prerequisite for leaders as they face more stressful situations with added responsibilities of managing teams, projects, and customers. A good leader always has good EQ along with IQ. A leader with low EQ will not be able to cope with challenges leading to yelling, screaming, and emotional outburst. This will lead to bad decisions and communication failure within team ultimately affecting the project, business, and morale of the team members.

Jamie Dimon, chairman and CEO of JPMorgan Chase, is a very good example of an emotional intelligent CEO. He firmly believes in practicing EI and has quoted, *'I believe social intelligence and "emotional quotient", or EQ, matter in management. EQ can include empathy, clarity of thought, compassion, and strength of character.'* In addition, the hiring process in JPMorgan is very selective as Jamie Dimon places huge importance on selecting people with EI traits like relatability and good character.

Emotional intelligence also affects our stress levels and anxiety. In other words, high EQ means decrease in stress levels and better quality of life. Cultivating emotional maturity will help you manage your emotion that in turn makes you more self-aware and calm. The social skills aspect of EI will help you better express and communicate with others, ensuring healthy professional and social relationships. The self-awareness and social awareness helps you lead your live consciously in the present and improve your quality of life.

People are accepting EI in the mainstream and considering it as important as 'regular' intelligence (measured as intelligence quotient [IQ]). Organizations are realizing the importance of high EQ and are giving it weightage during hiring and promoting a candidate. If two job candidates have similar qualification, IQ, and talent, the one who is perceived as having a higher EQ will likely be hired by the organization.

How do we build emotional intelligence?

We have realized the importance of emotional intelligence and also that the emotional intelligence traits can be learnt and master with continuous practice. So how do we go about it? Dr Travis Bradberry and Jean Greaves in their book *Emotional Intelligence 2.0* take the concept popularized by Daniel Goleman and expand it further. According to this, our emotional intelligence consists of four core skills: self-awareness, self-management, social awareness, and relationship management.

Self-awareness and self-management fall under the category of personal competence. The focus here is on managing our own emotions as well as our behaviors. Increase your self-awareness by paying attention to the present moment and being aware of your emotions. We live in a hyper busy world, moving from one task to another throughout the day, our emotions are put in the back burner, and our responses to situations are reactive, i.e., we simply react to problems commonly called firefighting. Instead, if we increase our self-awareness and check in with our emotions at regular intervals during the day, our responses will be 'proactive'. With proactive thinking, you will be able to anticipate the problems and provide an effective response. This will help boost your self-confidence and your self-worth. It has been proven beyond doubt that self-awareness helps in mastering your emotions and being calm and more centered. Stress management techniques like mindfulness and meditation also help in increasing awareness.

The next logical step is to ensure that our emotions are influencing our behavior positively so that we can be a better version of ourselves. Emotions and behaviors are interlinked. This is self-regulation or 'self-management'. The lack of this leads to undesirable behaviors and negative consequences. Be honest in evaluating your own behavior in different situations; build the self-discipline to manage negative behavior as and when it's identified. Along with this emotional self-control, adaptability or adaptive coping is also one of the key skills in self-management. Change is constant. Instead of fighting the inevitable, being flexible and looking at things realistically and objectively will go a long way in increasing your EQ.

It's understood that in addition to managing our own emotions, EI skills include the ability to recognize and understand the emotions, needs, and concerns of other people. This skill influences the way you handle relationships. This falls under the social competence category, which includes 'social awareness' and 'relationship management'. Increase your social awareness skills by improving your empathy. Empathy is to understand others' point of views, feelings, and perspectives. Applying the age-old quote 'put yourself in his/her shoe' is a good way to begin empathizing more. This is very important for success as pointed out by Stephen Covey in his book *7 Habits of Highly Effective People'*. Habit 5 is 'Seek First to Understand Than to Be Understood', i.e., empathy.

Improving your communication skills especially listening skills is a huge part of relationship management as it makes a positive impact on the quality of your relationships. Practicing 'active listening' helps increase EQ. Active listening technique helps build an effective two-way communication. This includes making a conscious effort to listen and understand the other person, keeping the focus on the other person by making eye contact while talking, paying attention to nonverbal cues such as body language, and paraphrasing to assure the other person of your interest.

In addition, good communication skills help in conflict resolution. Conflicts are bound to happen when two people work or live together. Resolving conflicts in a constructive manner strengthens relationship and builds trust among people. Emotional intelligence is a vast subject, and working on improving it is a life-long process. It's very important to practice the techniques discussed to see any improvement in EQ.

Increase your emotional intelligence by
- self-awareness and self-management - respond to situations, not react!
- social awareness and relationship management - active listening and empathy.

STRESS MANAGEMENT

It's not stress that kills us, it is our reaction to it.
—Hans Selye

What is stress management?

In this day and age, stress management has become a buzzword. Before we get to manage the stress, let's understand what stress is. Stress is a physical body response to help us cope with difficult and challenging environment/situations. Stress is not necessarily a bad word; it is essential for our survival, and in the short term, it will help you grow and perceive a challenging environment as an opportunity. This may lead to a favorable outcome. It's called a positive stress or eustress. However, in the long term and beyond the individual stress tolerance point, it becomes negative stress or distress. This decreases productivity and leads to anxiety and health problems.

During stress, the body releases a host of hormones, including adrenaline and cortisol. This 'fight or flight' stress response of the body helps to deal with the perceived threat. Adrenaline increases the heart rate and boosts the energy supplies that the body needs during stress. Cortisol also called the stress hormone, which in right amounts help regulate metabolism and blood pressure. However, long-term continuous exposure to cortisol due to the activation of our body stress response system leads to anxiety, depression, heart disease, and various other health problems.

Stress management is all about understanding and practicing techniques to control the stress levels in our body. This is imperative for our everyday functioning, maintaining overall health and happiness.

Stress can be both positive or negative
- Positive stress leads to opportunities and favorable outcomes
- Negative stress leads to anxiety and health problems

Why do we need stress management?

Experts have identified that 'stress management' is one of the keys to productivity and successful career. To understand this further, let's look at the most frequently used analogy: the body's stress response system is like an alarm system, which goes 'on' when a threat is perceived. The body returns to its normal state after the perceived threat is elapsed. However, with our busy lives, one task leads to the next, keeping the alarm system, i.e., stress response system, active. This leads to long-term chronic stress and is harmful to the overall well-being of a person.

This leads to the next question: what is considered a threat? A threat in this case is called a stressor, an event that triggers the stress response system. Stressors are highly individualistic. There are multiple stressors in our modern life. It could be major life changes (death, divorce), family and social demands (earning enough money, maintaining good relationships), personal expectations (getting good grades), daily stress (driving in peak traffic). The effects of these stressors on people vary. Some people are able to handle major life changes with minimum impact, while others falter with daily stressors. Using stress management tools and techniques help us to better cope with these stressors.

The negative effect of stress affects the physical as well as psychological aspects of a person. Stress is an active cause in diseases like obesity, heart disease, diabetes, and high blood pressure. Hence, it's really important to pay attention to body signals to understand and reduce stress. Self-awareness helps you observe your body reaction to the stressors. The following are some of the early warning signs of stress. Recognizing it is the first step in being able to manage the stress before it turns into a major health problem.

- Frequent headaches during the day
- Difficulty falling asleep or staying asleep, i.e., sleep disturbances
- Muscle tension, especially neck or back
- Restless/anxious/irritable
- Difficulty in concentrating, loss of energy
- Overeating comfort foods (stress eating), loss of appetite
- Alcohol/tobacco addiction

Understanding your emotions and mental state is as important as listening to your body signals because stress has psychological side effects as well. It can impact your thoughts, feelings, and behavior. Stress that's left unchecked can lead to depression, panic attacks, and anxiety. Given all these serious implications of stress symptoms, it is abundantly clear that we need to use stress management techniques so that the body can learn to deactivate the stress response system and return to the normal healthy state after a stressor is ceased.

How to manage stress?

As a matter of fact, stress is a part of our lives, and it is ongoing. It has become habitual to keep thinking, planning, and rehearsing the to-dos in our subconscious mind. The only way out is to empower ourselves with tools and techniques to handle it better. The most popular technique is meditation. The definition of *meditation* is 'the act of giving your attention to only one thing, either as a religious activity or as a way of becoming calm and relaxed'. In simple terms, meditation is a practice used to transform and quiet your mind. It involves conscious focus on a sound, image, object, breath, or feeling for a certain amount of time. With regular practice, you can zone out the distractions and achieve inner stillness, relaxation, and clarity. In addition, it helps reduce stress and tensions.

There are different types of mediation like transcendental meditation, guided visualization, Vipassana meditation, Raja yoga meditation, etc. It's *not* a one-size-fits-all kind of deal. Depending on your personality, inclination, and comfort level, you will have to try a few meditations before deciding what works best for you. The duration of the meditation is also individualistic. With regular practice, you can see a marked difference in your mental and emotional well-being.

Mindfulness is a type of meditation that is easy to practice and readily available for us. When you are mindful, you are paying attention to the present moment without any judgements. All of us have the capacity to *be* fully alert or aware in our environment and with what we are doing. However, our mind has a tendency to wander, run off with thoughts. If this happens, you have to bring the mind back to the present in a nonjudgmental, gentle manner. Pioneers in this field like Thich Nhat Hanh, global spiritual leader, and Jon Kabat-Zinn, American professor, have provided many techniques to improve our mindfulness and reduce stress.

Use of simple techniques like mindful breathing and walking mindfully have also proven to be beneficial with regular practice. 'Mindful breathing' is simply being aware of your breath. While breathing, just identify and say to yourself, 'This is an in-breath, this is an out-breath.' In addition to breathing, walking mindfully aids to center our mind and body. In simple terms, this means focusing your complete attention on walking slowly.

Being present, i.e., in the moment during day-to-day activities like eating, washing up, breathing, walking, etc., is a good opportunity to incorporate mindfulness. This brings the mind back to yourself and enhances the ability to respond to everyday challenges. 'Practice is important' to all meditation techniques. Without regular practice, it's futile to wish for results.

Exercise or any other physical activity should be on the top of your list, if you are serious about stress reduction. Even walking for thirty minutes serves a good stress reliever as the body releases feel-good endorphin hormones while exercising. This helps you to sleep better, improve your mood, and reduce the symptoms associated with depression and anxiety.

> Be present and take mini breaks to
> reduces stress during the day.

Apart from meditation, mindfulness, and exercise, simple changes in our everyday lives can help reduce stress. Taking mini breaks during the course of the workday will help you get a new perspective and also improve productivity. Social support is also very important especially while dealing with major life stressors. Talking to a trusted friend or joining support groups will provide comfort and relief.

Stress management is a vast subject, and there are numerous studies conducted to identify new techniques to help us deal with it. The latest research by Kelly McGonigal, a health psychologist and lecturer at Stanford University, focuses on how to make stress your friend. According to her, believing that stress is beneficial to you even when you are under a lot of stress can actually reduce the harmful effects of stress.

Positive attitude and the continued practice of stress management techniques can make you calmer, happier, and more efficient. Isn't it what we all want?

AUTHOR'S NOTE

'To have it all' is the latest success mantra. Personal contentment as well as career success is the elusive unicorn that we all chase. This need not be brushed aside as an impossible goal. Planning, prioritization, and using the tips discussed in this book will definitely help make it a reality.

This book is an amalgamation of the lessons I learnt in life, my background in computer science and in the IT industry. I have worked for eighteen years in this industry, including as founder and director of two startups. I have picked up a few lessons on the way; I will be the first to admit that I had to learn some things the hard way. Over time, I have realized the importance of these lessons, and hence, the book. Brainstorming with my colleagues/friends about their regrets and successes has added to the book's content.

This book is designed to be a quick read in this fast-paced world. However, just reading this book will not suffice; these topics need to be implemented in your everyday life. Furthermore, the research for these topics is included in the further reading section. Perusing these will definitely be beneficial in the long run.

ALL THE VERY BEST!

'Success doesn't come to you, you go to it.'
—Marva Collins

Suman V R

FURTHER READINGS

Networking

1. Web references:
   - LinkedIn: https://news.linkedin.com/2017/6/eighty-percent-of-professionals-consider-networking-important-to-career-success
   - Richard Branson, Virgin: https://www.virgin.com/entrepreneur/richard-branson-why-you-should-network
2. Book reference:
   - Martin Yate: *Knock 'em Dead Social Networking: For Job Search and Professional Success*

Know Your Strengths

1. Web references:
   Understanding self-actualization: Maslow's hierarchy of needs https://positivepsychologyprogram.com/self-actualization/

Standardized tests websites:
   - Myers-Briggs Foundation: http://www.myersbriggs.org/
   - Gallup's Strengths Finder Test: https://www.gallupstrengthscenter.com/home/en-us/strengthsfinder?utm_source=strengthsfinder&utm_campaign=coming_soon&utm_medium=redirect
   - Richard Step: http://richardstep.com/richardstep-strengths-weaknesses-aptitude-test/

2. Book references:
- Robert Kaplan: *What You're Really Meant To Do: A Roadmap for Reaching Your Unique Potential*
- Marcus Buckingham: *Discover Your Strengths*

Personal Planning

1. Web references:
   - Small Business Statistics: https://www.businessinsider.com/why-small-businesses-fail-infographic-2017-8?IR=T
   - SMART goals: https://www.techrepublic.com/article/use-smart-goals-to-launch-management-by-objectives-plan/

Time Management

1. Web references:
- Eisenhower's urgent/important principle: https://www.mindtools.com/pages/article/newHTE_91.htm http://www.eisenhower.me/eisenhower-matrix/

- Statistics: https://www.statista.com/statistics/433871/daily-social-media-usage-worldwide/

Emotional Intelligence

1. Web references:
- EQ tests details – Mayer-Salovey-Caruso Emotional Intelligence Test (MSCEIT): http://langleygroup.com.au/work/msceit/
- The Emotional Quotient Inventory 2.0 (EQ-i 2.0): http://www.eiconsortium.org/measures/eqi.html
- Jamie Dimon's take on a good leader: https://www.chase.com/news/111614-jamie-dimon-hallmarks-of-a-good-leader

2. Book references:
- Daniel Goleman: *Emotional Intelligence: Why It Can Matter More Than IQ* (1995)
- Dr Travis Bradberry and Jean Greaves: *Emotional Intelligence 2.0*

Stress Management

1. Web references:
- Kelly Mcgonigal: 'How to make stress your friend?' https://www.ted.com/talks/kelly_mcgonigal_how_to_make_stress_your_friend?language=en

2. Book references:
- Jon Kabat-Zinn: *Wherever You Go, There You Are*
- Thich Nhat Hanh: *Making Space*